Baby and Me

Baby Record Book

Hello You!

Here is a picture of you in Mummy's tummy at ..... weeks.

Place scan photo here

The day Mummy and Daddy found out they were expecting was _____

_____

Mummy felt _____

Daddy felt _____

The first people they shared the happy news with were _____

_____

You were due to arrive on _____

_____

Twinkle, Twinkle, Little Star

Twinkle, twinkle, little star,
How I wonder what you are!
Up above the world so high,
Like a diamond in the sky.

When the blazing sun is gone,
When he nothing shines upon,
Then you show your little light,
Twinkle, twinkle all the night.

Then the traveller in the dark,
Thanks you for your tiny spark,
He could not see which way to go,
If you did not twinkle so.

In the dark blue sky you keep,
And often through my curtains peep,
For you never shut your eye,
Till the sun is in the sky.

As your bright and tiny spark,
Lights the traveller in the dark,
Though I know not what you are,
Twinkle, twinkle, little star.

Hello World!

Place newborn photo here

All About You

You were born on _____ at (time) _____

You were born at (place) _____

You weighed _____

You measured (length) _____

Your hair was _____ and your eyes were _____

Present at your birth was/were _____

Your First Weeks

You came home on --

Your first visitors were --

People said you looked like --

You were soothed by --

Memorable moments: --

Here you are at just a few weeks old...

Place photo here

Round and Round the Garden

Round and round the garden,

Like a teddy bear;

(Draw a circle on the palm of your
baby's hand with your finger)

One step, two steps,

(Walk your fingers up your baby's arm)

Tickle you under there!

(Tickle baby under the arm)

Lavender's Blue

Lavender's blue, dilly, dilly,
Lavender's green;
When I am king, dilly, dilly,
You shall be queen.

1 to 2 Months Old

The lovely things you do now _____

The sweet sounds you make _____

How well you are feeding _____

What you think of bath time _____

Your weight .... and height .... at 2 months.

So Adorable...

Place photo here

2 to 4 Months Old

The new things you can do _____

Places we love to go _____

Friends we see _____

Your favourite toys, books and games _____

How you are sleeping now _____

Your weight ....
and height ....
at 4 months.

Cute as a Button

Place photo here

Row, Row, Row Your Boat

Row, row, row your boat
Gently down the stream.
Merrily, merrily, merrily, merrily,
Life is but a dream.

Hey Diddle Diddle

Hey diddle diddle, the cat and the fiddle,
The cow jumped over the moon.
The little dog laughed to see such fun
And the dish ran away with the spoon!

4 to 6 Months Old

The things that make you laugh _____

The funny sounds you make _____

Your favourite bedtime toy _____

The most adorable thing you do _____

Your weight ....
and height ....
at 6 months.

Wonderful You...

Place photo here

6 to 9 Months Old

The clever (and mischievous!) things you can do now ....

Your favourite foods ....

Your hair is now ....

Your weight ....
and height ....
at 8 months.

Sleepy Times...

Place photo here

Baa, Baa, Black Sheep

Baa, baa, black sheep,
Have you any wool?
Yes sir, yes sir,
Three bags full.

One for the master,
One for the dame,
And one for the little boy
Who lives down the lane.

This Little Piggy

This little piggy went to market,

(Wiggle 'big' toe)

This little piggy stayed at home,

(Wiggle 'long' toe)

This little piggy had roast beef,

(Wiggle 'middle' toe)

This little piggy had none,

(Wiggle 'ring' toe)

And this little piggy cried,

"Wee, wee, wee!"

all the way home.

(Wiggle 'pinky' toe and tickle bottom of foot!)

9 to 12 Months Old

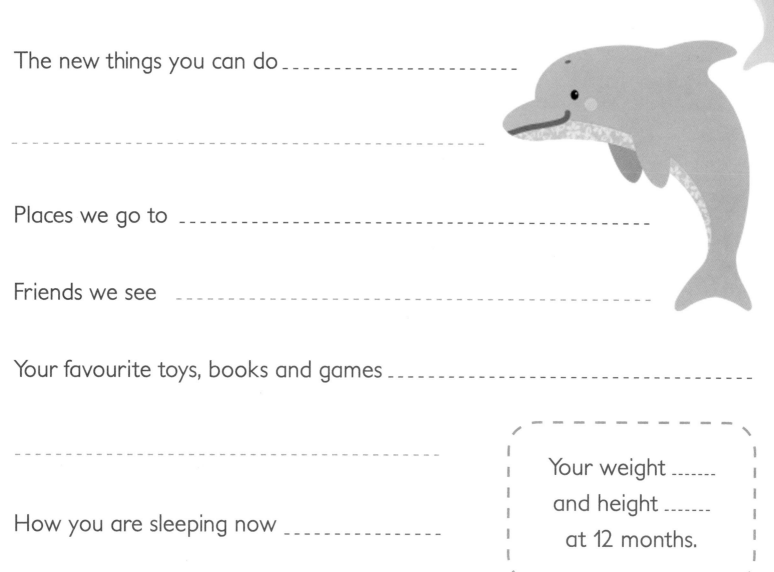

The new things you can do _

_ _

Places we go to _

Friends we see _

Your favourite toys, books and games _ _ _ _ _ _ _ _ _ _ _ _ _ _ _ _ _

_ _

How you are sleeping now _ _ _ _ _ _ _ _ _ _ _ _ _ _

Your weight _ _ _ _ _ _ _
and height _ _ _ _ _ _ _
at 12 months.

Special Times

Place photo here

Your First Birthday!

How we celebrated _____

What you wore _____

What we ate _____

The best memories of your special day _____

_____

_____

_____

Happy Birthday!

Place birthday photo here

Memorable Milestones

You first rolled over aged ....

You first sat up aged ....

You first crawled aged ....

We discovered your first tooth at ....

Your first word was ....

You took your first steps aged ....

You had your first haircut ....